Living Room

Designs by Sandra Miller Maxfield

Size: **Corner Chair:** 6¼ inches W x 5¾ inches H x 4 inches D (15.9cm x 14.6cm x 10.2cm)
Love Seats: 8 inches W x 5¾ inches H x 3½ inches D (20.3cm x 14.6cm x 8.9cm)
Table: 3⅞ inches square x 2¾ inches H (9.8cm x 7cm)
Pillows: 2⅜ inches square (6cm)

Skill Level: Intermediate

Materials

❑ 5 sheets 7-count plastic canvas
❑ Red Heart Super Saver Art. E300 medium weight yarn as listed in color key
❑ #16 tapestry needle
❑ Small amount of fiberfill or plastic canvas scraps

Stitching Step by Step

Corner Chair

1 Following graphs (pages 4 and 5) throughout, cut one each of the following from plastic canvas for corner chair: backrest (A), cushion (B), front (D), back (F) and base (G). Cut two sides (C) and two gussets (E). Base (G) will remain unstitched.

2 Stitch remaining corner chair pieces following graphs. Leave bottom portion on backrest (A) unstitched as indicated.

3 Following Fig. 1 (page 5) and using white through step 4, Whipstitch one short end of two gusset (E) pieces together. Whipstitch backrest (A) to cushion (B) where indicated with blue lines, easing as necessary to fit.

4 Whipstitch sides (C) to front (D); Whipstitch sides (C) and front (D) to cushion (B). Whipstitch gusset (E) to backrest (A); Whipstitch gusset (E) to back (F). Whipstitch assembled chair to unstitched base (G).

Love Seats

1 Following graphs (pages 4, 5 and 6) throughout, cut two each of the following from plastic canvas for love seats: backrest (A), cushion (H), front (I), short side (C), armrest side (J), armrest (K) and back (M). Cut four gussets (E) and four armrest braces (L). Cut two 43-hole x 23-hole pieces for love seat bases (N). Armrest braces (L) and bases (N) will remain unstitched.

2 Stitch remaining love seat pieces following graphs, leaving bottom portion on backrest (A) and armrest (K) unstitched as indicated.

3 Using white through step 8, Overcast inside edges of armrest braces (L) from blue dot to blue dot.

4 *Left love seat:* Following Fig. 2 (page 5) throughout assembly, Whipstitch one short end of two gusset (E) pieces together. Whipstitch one backrest (A) to one cushion (H) where indicated with blue lines.

5 Whipstitch one front (I) to cushion (H). On right side of love seat, Whipstitch one short side (C) to cushion (H) and to front (I).

6 On left side, with right sides facing, Whipstitch cushion (H) to one armrest (K) where indicated with orange lines. Starting at the bottom, Whipstitch outside edge of one armrest brace (L) to front (I), armrest side (J) and armrest (K). Continue Whipstitching armrest (K) and armrest brace (L) together to end of brace.

7 Starting at the bottom, Whipstitch outside edge of a second armrest brace (L) to armrest side (J), backrest (A), armrest (K) and gusset (E). Continue Whipstitching armrest (K) and armrest brace (L) together to end of brace; Overcast remaining edges of armrest (K).

8 Continue Whipstitching gusset (E) to backrest (A), catching short side (C) in Whipstitching on right side

of love seat. Whipstitch gusset (E) to back (M). Whipstitch assembled love seat to one unstitched base (N).

9 *Right love seat:* Whipstitch together following steps 4–8, reversing positions of sides.

Lamp

1 Cut lamp shade sections (O) and lamp base pieces (S) following graphs (page 3). Cut one 11-hole x 58-hole piece for lamp pole (P), five 2-hole x 58-hole pieces for lamp pole supports (Q), and one 7-hole x 7-hole piece for lamp pole top (R). Lamp pole supports (Q) will remain unstitched.

2 Stitch lamp pole (P) with white Continental Stitches. Following Fig. 3 through step 5, place five lamp pole supports (Q) together. Whipstitch 58-hole edges of lamp pole (P) together with supports (Q) inside, allowing two to three holes of supports (Q) to protrude from bottom edge of pole (P).

3 Stitch lamp shade sections (O) following graph. Using buff throughout, Overcast top edges from blue dot to blue dot and bottom edges from orange dot to orange dot. Whipstitch side edges togethe between blue dots and orange dots, forming shade (O).

4 Stitch lamp pole top (R) with white Continenta Stitches; Overcast edges. Using white through ste 5, center top (R) over pole (P) and tack in place. Tac corners of top (R) inside shade (O).

5 Place the four base (S) pieces together and stitch a one; Overcast outside edges. With ends of suppor (Q) inside center hole of base (S), Whipstitch bottom edg of pole (P) to cutout edges of base (S).

Pillows

1 Cut pillow pieces from plastic canvas according to graphs (pages 3 and 4).

2 Stitch two solid pillow pieces with frosty green as graphed. Stitch remaining two pieces with buff. Place wrong sides of corresponding pieces together, making sure rows of Slanted Gobelin Stitches are going the same direction.

Whipstitch together, filling with fiberfill or plastic canvas scraps before closing.

3 Stitch two striped pillow pieces with buff and white as graphed. Stitch two pieces replacing buff with frosty green. Stitch remaining two pieces replacing white with frosty green. Place wrong sides of corresponding pieces together, making sure stripes are going the same direction. Whipstitch together, filling with fiberfill or plastic canvas scraps before closing.

Table

1 Cut table top and legs from plastic canvas according to graphs (below).

2 Stitch pieces following graphs.

3 Using white, Whipstitch side edges of legs together. Using buff, Whipstitch table top to top edges of legs. Overcast remaining edges of legs with white.

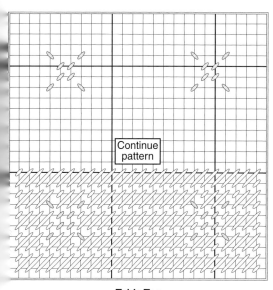

Table Top
25 holes x 25 holes
Cut 1

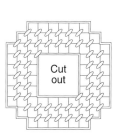

Lamp Base (S)
10 holes x 10 holes
Cut 4
Stitch as 1

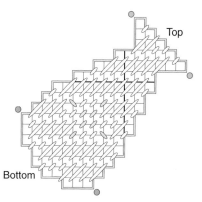

Lamp Shade Section (O)
16 holes x 16 holes
Cut 6

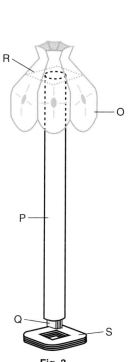

Fig. 3
Lamp Assembly Diagram

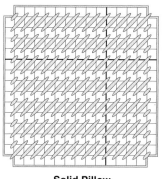

Solid Pillow
15 holes x 15 holes
Cut 4
Stitch 2 as graphed
Stitch 2 with buff

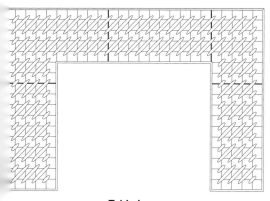

Table Legs
25 holes x 17 holes
Cut 4

COLOR KEY

Yards	Medium Weight Yarn
300 (274.3m)	☐ White #311
48 (43.9m)	☐ Buff #334
44 (40.3m)	☐ Frosty green #661

Color numbers given are for Red Heart Super Saver Art. E300 medium weight yarn.

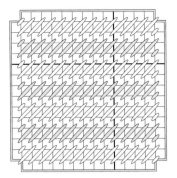

Striped Pillow
15 holes x 15 holes
Cut 6
Stitch 2 as graphed
Stitch 2 replacing buff
with frosty green
Stitch 2 replacing white
with frosty green

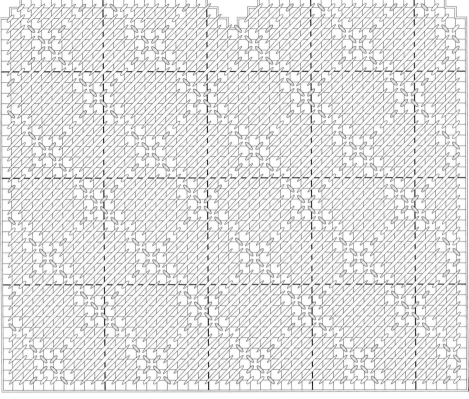

Corner Chair Back (F)
45 holes x 37 holes
Cut 1

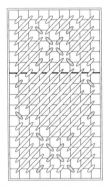

Corner Chair Front (D)
9 holes x 16 holes
Cut 1

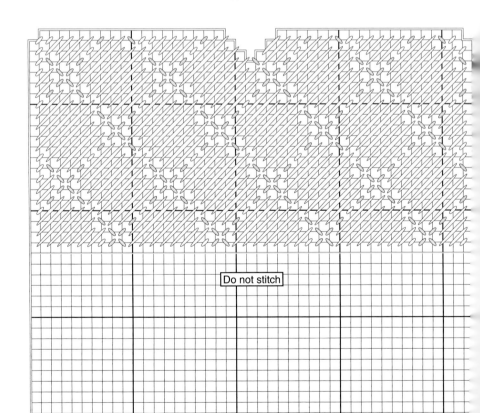

Do not stitch

Corner Chair & Love Seat Backrest (A)
43 holes x 37 holes
Cut 1 for corner chair
Cut 2 for love seats

Corner Chair Side (C)
20 holes x 16 holes
Cut 2

Love Seat Short Side (C)
20 holes x 16 holes
Cut 2

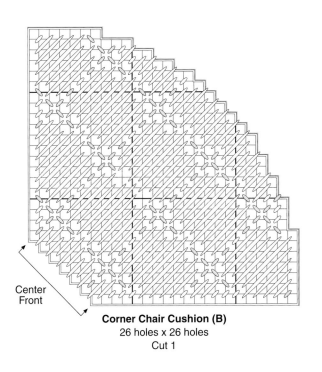

Corner Chair Cushion (B)
26 holes x 26 holes
Cut 1

Center
Front

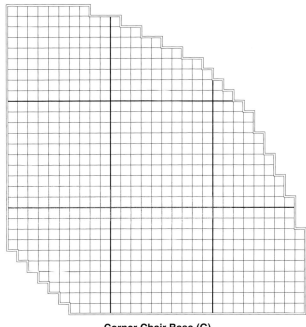

Corner Chair Base (G)
29 holes x 29 holes
Cut 1
Do not stitch

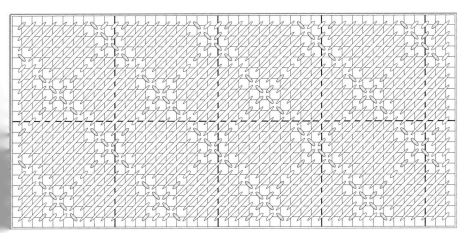

Love Seat Cushion (H)
43 holes x 20 holes
Cut 2

Stitch left love seat as shown
Stitch right love seat switching
K, J and L with C

Continue pattern

Gusset (E)
3 holes x 59 holes
Cut 2 for corner chair
Cut 4 for love seats

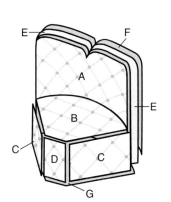

Fig. 1
Corner Chair Assembly Diagram

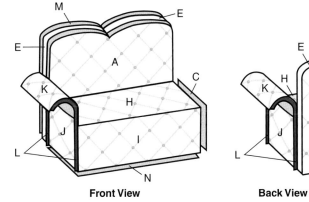

Front View   Back View

Fig. 2
Love Seat Assembly Diagram

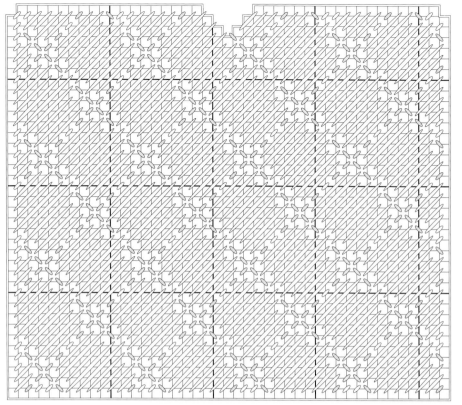

Love Seat Back (M)
43 holes x 37 holes
Cut 2

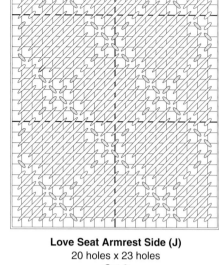

Love Seat Armrest Side (J)
20 holes x 23 holes
Cut 2

Inside
Edge

**Love Seat
Armrest Brace (L)**
7 holes x 25 holes
Cut 4
Do not stitch

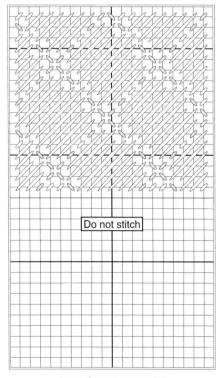

Do not stitch

Love Seat Armrest (K)
20 holes x 34 holes
Cut 2

COLOR KEY

Yards	Medium Weight Yarn
300 (274.3m)	☐ White #311
48 (43.9m)	☐ Buff #334
44 (40.3m)	☐ Frosty green #661

Color numbers given are for Red Heart Super Saver Art. E300 medium weight yarn.

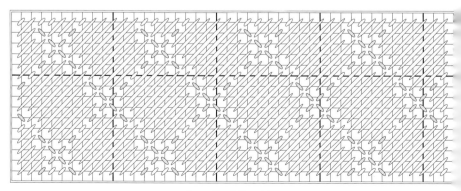

Love Seat Front (I)
43 holes x 16 holes
Cut 2

Patio

Designs by Carolyn Christmas

Size: **Sofa:** 6¼ inches W x 5⅜ inches H x
2⅞ inches D (15.9cm x 13.7cm x 7.3cm),
including cushion
Chairs: 2¾ inches W x 5⅜ inches H x
2¾ inches D (7cm x 13.7cm x 7cm),
including cushions
Coffee Table: 5½ inches W x 2⅛ inches H x
2⅞ inches D (14cm x 5.4cm x 7.3cm),
including cover
End Table: 2¾ inches W x 2⅝ inches H x
2¾ inches D (7cm x 6.7cm x 7cm),
including cover
Pillows: 1½ inches square (3.8cm)
Skill Level: Intermediate

Materials

❏ 3 sheets white 7-count plastic canvas
❏ Plastic canvas yarn as listed in color key
❏ #16 tapestry needle
❏ Small amount of fiberfill or yarn scraps
❏ Hot-glue gun or craft glue

Stitching Step by Step

Sofa & Chairs

1 Cut sofa back and front, chair backs and fronts, sofa seat, chair seat, sofa and arm chair sides, and side chair sides from plastic canvas according to graphs (pages 10 and 11), cutting away gray areas on back, front and side pieces, and cutout area on arm chair and sofa side pieces. Sofa front, chair fronts, sofa and arm chair sides, and side chair sides will remain unstitched.

2 Stitch sofa back, sofa seat, chair backs and chair seats following graphs, being careful to not run yarn behind unstitched areas.

3 *Sofa:* Using white through step 4, Overcast around side and top edges of back from blue dot to blue dot. Overcast edges of two sofa sides from blue dot to arrow on front edge. Whipstitch seat to bar indicated with blue line on sofa back graph. Whipstitch seat to bar indicated with arrows on sofa sides. Whipstitch sofa seat to top edge of sofa front.

4 Whipstitch sides to back from blue dots to bottom of legs, forming back corners of sofa. Whipstitch sides to front from seat to bottom of legs.

5 *Arm chair:* Repeat steps 3 and 4, using two arm chair sides and one each of chair back, chair seat and chair front.

6 *Side chair:* Using white, Overcast around side and top edges of remaining chair back from red dot to red dot. Whipstitch seat to bar indicated with blue line on chair back graph. Whipstitch seat to side chair sides and to chair front.

7 Whipstitch back to sides from red dots to bottom of legs, forming back corners of chair. Whipstitch sides to front from seat to bottom of legs.

Tables

1 Cut table covers, end table sides, and coffee table sides and ends according to graphs, cutting away gray areas on table sides and ends. Cut one 16-hole x 16-hole piece for end table top and one 34-hole x 16-hole piece for coffee table top. Table tops, sides and ends will remain unstitched.

2 Stitch and Overcast table covers following graphs, being careful to not run yarn behind unstitched areas.

3 Using white through step 4, Whipstitch coffee table sides to coffee table ends; Whipstitch sides and ends to coffee table top.

4 Whipstitch end table sides together; Whipstitch sides to end table top.

5 Place covers on corresponding table tops.

Pillows & Cushions

1 Cut throw pillows and cushion top and bottom pieces from plastic canvas according to graphs (pages 9 and 11). Cut two 41-hole x 1-hole pieces for sofa cushion sides, two 16-hole x 1-hole pieces for sofa cushion ends, and eight 16-hole x 1-hole pieces for chair cushion sides. Cushion bottom, side and end pieces will remain unstitched.

2 Stitch pillows and cushion tops following graphs, being careful to not run yarn behind unstitched areas on cushion tops.

3 For each of the three pillows, Whipstitch wrong sides of two pillow pieces together with white, stuffing with fiberfill or yarn scraps before closing.

4 Using frosty green throughout, Whipstitch sofa cushion top, bottom, sides and ends together. For each chair cushion, Whipstitch one top, one bottom and four sides together.

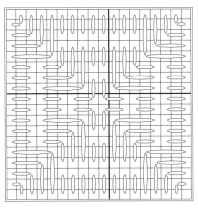

End Table Cover
18 holes x 18 holes
Cut 1

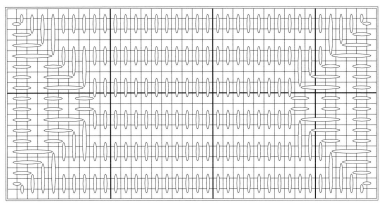

Coffee Table Cover
36 holes x 18 holes
Cut 1

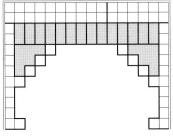

Coffee Table End
16 holes x 12 holes
Cut 2,
cutting away gray areas
Do not stitch

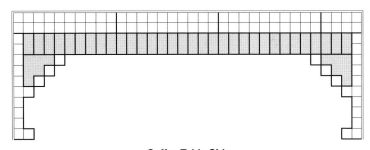

Coffee Table Side
34 holes x 12 holes
Cut 2,
cutting away gray areas
Do not stitch

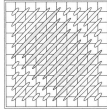

Throw Pillow
10 holes x 10 holes
Cut 6

COLOR KEY	
Yards	**Plastic Canvas Yarn**
43 (39.4m)	☐ White
22 (20.2m)	☐ Frosty green

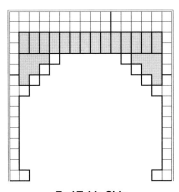

End Table Side
16 holes x 16 holes
Cut 4,
cutting away gray areas
Do not stitch

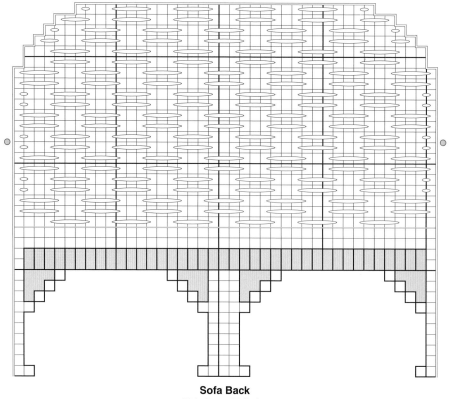

Sofa Back
41 holes x 35 holes
Cut 1,
cutting away gray areas

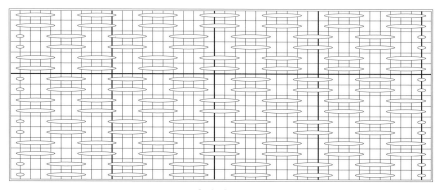

Sofa Seat
41 holes x 16 holes
Cut 1

COLOR KEY	
Yards	**Plastic Canvas Yarn**
43 (39.4m)	☐ White
22 (20.2m)	☐ Frosty green

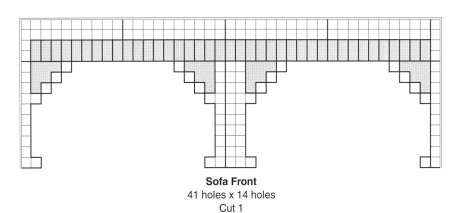

Sofa Front
41 holes x 14 holes
Cut 1
cutting away gray areas
Do not stitch

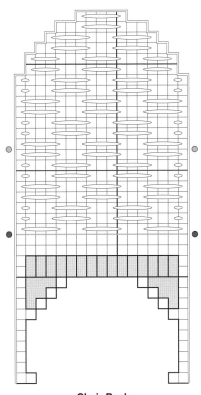

Chair Back
17 holes x 35 holes
Cut 1 for each chair
cutting away gray areas

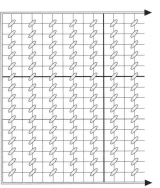

Chair Seat
17 holes x 16 holes
Cut 1 for each chair

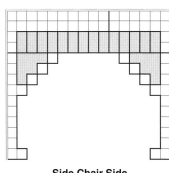

Side Chair Side
16 holes x 14 holes
Cut 2,
cutting away gray areas
Do not stitch

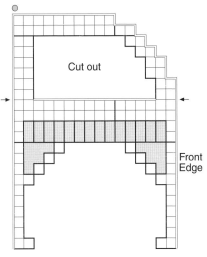

Cut out

Front
Edge

Sofa & Arm Chair Side
16 holes x 22 holes
Cut 2 for each,
cutting away gray areas
and cutout area
Do not stitch

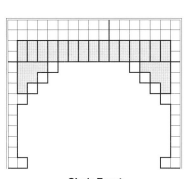

Sofa Cushion Top & Bottom
40 holes x 16 holes
Cut 2
Stitch top only

Chair Cushion Top & Bottom
16 holes x 16 holes
Cut 1 top & 1 bottom for each chair
Stitch top pieces only

Chair Front
17 holes x 14 holes
Cut 1 for each chair,
cutting away gray areas
Do not stitch

Picnic Set

Designs by Mickie Akins

Size: **Picnic Table:** 7 inches W x 4¼ inches H x 6⅝ inches D (17.8cm x 10.8cm x 16.8cm)
Grill: 5¼ inches W x 5⅛ inches H x 3⅝ inches D (13.3cm x 13cm x 9.2cm)

Skill Level: Intermediate

Materials

❑ 3 sheets clear stiff 7-count plastic canvas
❑ Small amount black 7-count plastic canvas
❑ Plastic canvas yarn as listed in color key
❑ #16 tapestry needle

Stitching Step by Step

Picnic Table

1 Cut two tops, two sides, four seats and six legs from clear plastic canvas according to graphs (pages 15 and 16), cutting out eight narrow holes on tops and two narrow holes on seats. Cut one large hole in each table leg where indicated. Also cut two 22-hole x 2-hole pieces from clear plastic canvas for table braces.

2 Using rust through step 6, work braces with Continental Stitches. Whipstitch one short end of the two braces together; Overcast long edges.

3 Stitch sides; Overcast bottom edges. For table top and each of the two seats, place two pieces of plastic canvas together and stitch as one. For each of the two table legs place three pieces together and stitch as one.

4 Overcast seats. Overcast all inner and outer edges of table top except outer edges within brackets. Overcast all inner and outer edges of legs except top edge and edges within rust brackets.

5 Following graphs and Fig. 1 (page 14) through step 6, Whipstitch top to sides within brackets. Whipstitch legs to sides within rust brackets.

6 Tack top to legs where indicated with blue lines. Tack seats to legs where indicated with green lines. With right side of assembled brace facing wrong side of legs, tack ends of brace to legs where indicated with red line; tack center of brace to center wrong side of table top.

Grill

1 From clear plastic canvas, cut four grill ends, four legs, three grill basin pieces, two leg braces, one hood top, one hood back, one hood front, one top shelf and one bottom shelf from clear plastic canvas according to graphs (pages 14 and 15).

2 Cut one grate from black plastic canvas according to graph (page 14), carefully cutting away yellow areas. Grate will remain unstitched.

3 Following graphs throughout, for each of the two legs, place two pieces of plastic canvas together and stitch as one. Beginning on left side, Overcast around side and bottom edges of front legs from blue dot to red arrow. Beginning on right side, Overcast around side and bottom edges of back legs from blue dot to green arrow. Top edges of legs will not be stitched at this time.

4 Stitch all remaining pieces. Overcast leg braces along diagonal edges from blue dot to blue dot.

5 Use black through step 9 unless otherwise instructed. Following Fig. 2 (page 14), Whipstitch basin pieces together along 22-hole edges; Whipstitch ends to basin, easing as necessary to fit. Whipstitch hood top and back together along 22-hole edges; Whipstitch hood front to hood top; Whipstitch ends to hood, easing as necessary to fit. Overcast bottom edges of hood ends and hood front, leaving bottom edge of hood back unstitched at this time.

6 Whipstitch leg braces to top shelf; Overcast edge on shelf between braces. Whipstitch bottom edge of hood back to bar indicated on grate with blue arrows.

7 Whipstitch top edge of basin right end to grate and top shelf, working through all three layers. Whipstitch top edge of basin left end to grate.

8 Whipstitch legs to grate, basin and top shelf, working through all layers; Whipstitch legs to leg braces.

9 Attach bottom shelf to legs where indicated with yellow lines. Overcast remaining edges of bottom shelf with rust.

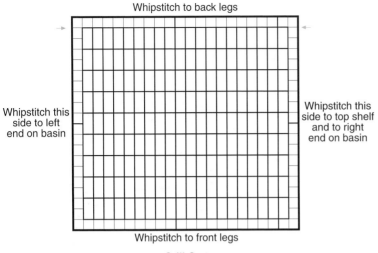

Whipstitch to back legs

Whipstitch this side to left end on basin

Whipstitch this side to top shelf and to right end on basin

Whipstitch to front legs

Grill Grate
22 holes x 20 holes
Cut 1 from black,
cutting away yellow areas
Do not stitch

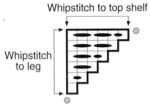

Whipstitch to top shelf

Whipstitch to leg

Grill Leg Brace
6 holes x 6 holes
Cut 2, reverse 1,
from clear

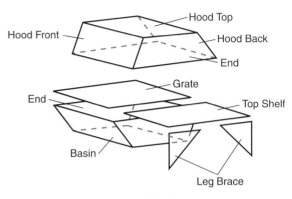

Hood Front — Hood Top — Hood Back — End

End — Grate — Top Shelf

Basin — Leg Brace

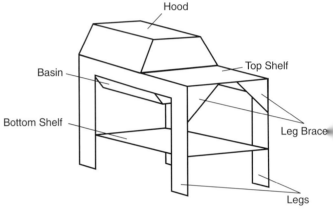

Hood

Basin — Top Shelf

Bottom Shelf — Leg Brace

Legs

Fig. 2

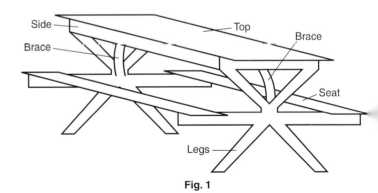

Side — Top — Brace

Brace — Seat

Legs

Fig. 1

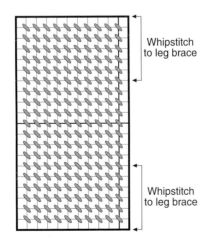

Whipstitch to leg brace

Whipstitch to leg brace

Grill Top Shelf
11 holes x 20 holes
Cut 1 from clear

COLOR KEY
Yards	Plastic Canvas Yarn
120 (110m)	Rust
60 (54.9m)	Black
	Attach top to table legs
	Attach seat to table legs
	Attach brace to table legs
	Attach bottom shelf to grill legs

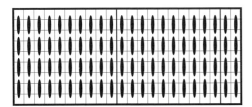

Grill Basin & Hood Front
22 holes x 9 holes
Cut 3 from clear
for grill basin
Cut 1 from clear
for grill hood front

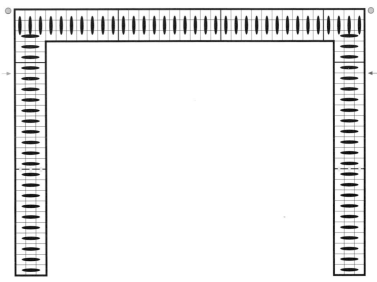

Grill Legs
34 holes x 25 holes
Cut 4 from clear
For each of the 2 legs, place
2 pieces together and stitch as 1

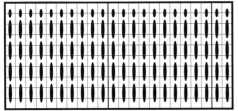

Whipstitch this edge on hood top
to top edge of hood front

Grill Hood Top & Back
22 holes x 10 holes
Cut 2 from clear

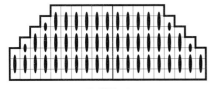

Grill End
19 holes x 7 holes
Cut 4

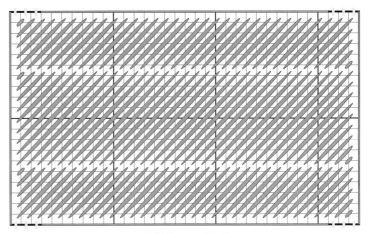

Grill Bottom Shelf
34 holes x 20 holes
Cut 1 from clear

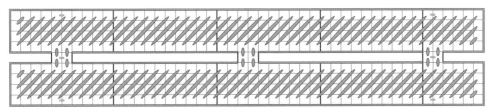

Table Seat
46 holes x 9 holes
Cut 4 from clear
For each seat, place 2
together and stitch as 1

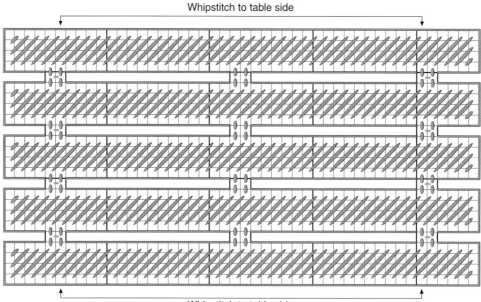

Whipstitch to table side

Whipstitch to table side

Table Top
46 holes x 24 holes
Cut 2 from clear
Stitch as 1

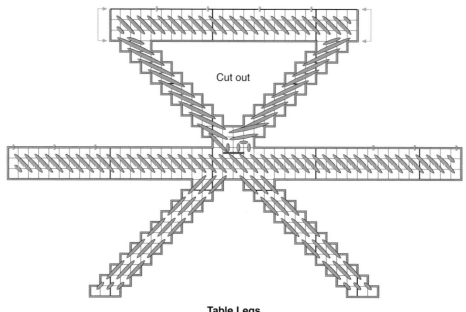

Cut out

Table Legs
44 holes x 27 holes
Cut 6 from clear
For each of the 2 legs, place
3 pieces together and stitch as 1

COLOR KEY

Yards	Plastic Canvas Yarn
120 (110m)	▨ Rust
60 (54.9m)	■ Black
	▬ Attach top to table legs
	▬ Attach seat to table legs
	▬ Attach brace to table legs
	▬ Attach bottom shelf to grill legs

Whipstitch to table top

Table Side
35 holes x 3 holes
Cut 2 from clear

Bedroom Suite

Designs by Celia Lange Designs

Size: **Canopy Bed:** 14⅝ inches W x 13⅜ inches H x
9¼ inches D (37.1cm x 34cm x 23.5cm)
Armoire: 7½ inches W x 12¾ inches H x
3½ inches D (19cm x 32.4cm x 8.9cm)
Dressing Screen: 9¾ inches W x 9½ inches H
(24.8cm x 24.1cm), not folded
Nightstand: 2⅝ inches W x 4½ inches H x
2⅝ inches D (6.7cm x 11.4cm x 6.7cm)
Lamp: 1¾ inches W x 3 inches H x
1¾ inches D (4.4cm x 7.6cm x 4.4cm)
Square Pillows: 2⅜ inches square (6cm)

Skill Level: Intermediate

Materials

- ❑ 9 sheets stiff 7-count plastic canvas
- ❑ ½ sheet 10-count plastic canvas
- ❑ Red Heart Super Saver Art. E300 medium weight yarn as listed in color key
- ❑ DMC 6-strand embroidery floss as listed in color key
- ❑ #16 tapestry needle
- ❑ #18 tapestry needle
- ❑ 2 yards (1.8m) ¼-inch/7mm-wide white satin ribbon
- ❑ 2 (6mm) white pearl beads
- ❑ 1 yard coordinating-color cotton fabric with tiny floral print
- ❑ ½ yard (0.5m) coordinating color net lace fabric
- ❑ 8½ x 11-inch/21.6 x 27.9cm-piece lightweight white poster board
- ❑ 41½ inches (105.4cm) 1½-inch/39mm-wide white ruffled eyelet
- ❑ 9 x 13 x 1-inch (22.9 x 33 x 2.5cm) piece of foam for mattress
- ❑ 7 inches (17.8cm) 5/16-inch (0.8cm) dowel
- ❑ Polyester fiberfill
- ❑ Plastic wrap
- ❑ Hand-sewing needle
- ❑ White thread (optional) and thread to match floral-print fabric.
- ❑ Fusible web
- ❑ Plastic bags (optional)
- ❑ Thick heavy book
- ❑ White craft glue
- ❑ Hot-glue gun

Project Notes

Use medium weight yarn and #16 tapestry needle with 7-count plastic canvas. Use 12 plies of 6-strand embroidery floss and #18 tapestry needle with 10-count plastic canvas.

Glue pads are areas of otherwise unstitched canvas onto which a small square is Continental Stitched. This area may be as small as three stitches by three stitches. When a piece of unworked canvas needs to be glued to something, stitching a small glue pad onto the piece will cause the glue to hold the pieces together more firmly.

When cutting pieces from plastic canvas, keep each set of pieces together in a plastic bag to keep them separate (canopy bed pieces in one bag, lamp pieces in another bag, etc.). This will help when assembling the pieces.

Stitching Step by Step

1 Cut lamp pieces from 10-count plastic canvas; cut all remaining pieces from 7-count plastic canvas according to graphs (pages 21–27). If desired, place cut pieces together in a labeled plastic bag (see third Project Note above).

2 For box spring, cut two 85-hole x 57-hole pieces for top and bottom, two 85 x 11-hole pieces for sides and two 57-hole x 11-hole pieces for ends from 7-count plastic canvas.

3 Using white, work four glue pads (see second Project Note on page 17) evenly spaced along box spring sides and three glue pads evenly spaced along box spring ends. Top and bottom will remain unstitched.

4 Cut four 5-hole x 5-hole pieces from 7-count plastic canvas for bedpost caps and four for bedpost bottoms. Following first Project Note throughout all stitching and assembly, work caps and bottoms with white Continental Stitches.

5 For each of the two pole brackets, place four pieces together; stitch and Overcast as one. Place two lamp base pieces together and stitch as one.

6 Stitch remaining pieces following graphs. Whe background stitching is completed, work Straigh Stitches on lamp shade pieces and Backstitches o bedposts and lamp body pieces.

7 Overcast cutout areas on dressing screen panels an armoire front. Overcast lamp base and false drawer.

Dressing Screen Assembly

1 Cut three 2⅝ x 7½-inch (6.7 x 19cm) pieces from white poster board and six from lace. Spread a thin layer of white craft glue on one side of each poster board. Position one piece of lace across each poster board and allow to dry under a heavy book, placing plastic wrap between lace and book to protect book from glue. When dry, repeat with other side of poster board; allow to dry.

2 Center and glue one poster board between openings on two dressing screen panels; Whipstitch outside edges of the two panels together. Repeat with remaining panels.

3 Whipstitch panels together in every other hole. Screen should fold slightly like a fan and stand on its own.

Armoire Assembly

1 Whipstitch sides, front, back and top together; Overcast remaining edges. Overcast doors with Braided Overcast Stitch (page 27).

2 Using hot glue through step 3, attach shelf inside armoire, where indicated with blue lines. Attach false drawer to front where indicated with red lines.

3 Center and glue pole brackets to sides inside armoire 1¼ inches (3.2cm) from top, with open end of brackets facing up. Place dowel in brackets and glue to secure.

4 For doorknobs, glue or use hand-sewing needle and white thread to sew white pearl beads to doors where indicated on graph.

5 Cut two 2½ x 7⅝-inch (6.4 x 19.4cm) pieces each from white poster board and floral-print fabric. Place a thin layer of white craft glue on poster board; position fabric on poster board, smoothing out any bubbles. Place book over fabric; allow to dry. With fabric facing front, center and hot glue poster board behind openings on doors.

6 Stitching in every other hole, Whipstitch side edges of doors to openings on armoire front where indicated with brackets.

Nightstand Assembly

1 Whipstitch nightstand sides together; Whipstitch sides to top. Overcast bottom of legs and shelf.

2 Hot glue shelf inside legs about 1½ inches (3.8cm) up from bottom of legs.

Lamp Assembly

1 Whipstitch body pieces together with white floss, easing as necessary to fit; Overcast bottom edges. Whipstitch lamp shade pieces together; Overcast top and bottom edges.

2 Using hot glue throughout, glue lamp shade support inside lamp shade where indicated with green lines. Slide lamp up inside lamp shade; glue and/or tack in place. Center and glue bottom of lamp to base.

Canopy Bed Assembly

1 For each of the four bedposts, Whipstitch four bedpost pieces together, then Whipstitch to one cap and one bottom.

2 Whipstitch wrong sides of headboard pieces together and wrong sides of footboard pieces together.

3 For side canopy rail, with wrong sides facing, Whipstitch long edges of top to long edges of inner and outer sides; Overcast remaining edges. Repeat for remaining side canopy rail and for end canopy rails.

4 Cut two 13-inch (33cm) lengths and two 7¾-inch (19.7cm) lengths of eyelet. Hot glue 13-inch (33cm) lengths to back sides of canopy outer sides along top edges, trimming as necessary to fit. Repeat with 7¾-inch (19.7cm) lengths, gluing to canopy outer ends.

5 Using white and a Braided Whipstitch, Whipstitch box spring sides to box spring ends, then Whipstitch sides and ends to box spring top and bottom.

6 Align bottom edges of box spring and headboard. Center headboard horizontally and glue in place. Repeat with footboard.

7 Align top and side edges of box spring and side skirts; glue in place. Glue four bedposts to corners, placing bottom of bedposts 1¼ inches (3.2cm) from bottom of box spring.

8 Cut four 7 x 13-inch (17.8 x 33cm) pieces floral-print fabric for canopy curtains. Use good selvedge edge for hem or create a hem with fusible web or by sewing. With right sides facing, fold piece in half lengthwise and fuse ½-inch (1.3cm) seam. Turn right side out, finger-press flat and glue behind eyelet on side rails of canopy.

9 Glue side and end canopy rails between bedposts, aligning top edges. Cut white satin ribbon in four equal lengths. Tie curtains to centers of bedposts with a ribbon bow.

Bedspread & Pillows

1 Whipstitch corresponding sides of square pillows together, stuffing with fiberfill before closing.

2 For bedspread, cut a 14 x 17-inch (35.6 x 43.2cm) piece floral-print fabric. Fuse a ½-inch hem all around. Place foam mattress on box spring and cover with bedspread, adjusting ends and sides as desired.

3 For fabric pillow, cut one 18 x 4-inch (45.8 x 10.2cm) piece floral-print fabric. Fold fabric in half with right sides facing so piece measures 9 x 4 inches (22.9 x 10.2cm). Sew a ¼-inch (0.6cm) seam along 9-inch (22.9cm) edges. Fold open end down ¼ inch (.6cm); finger-press or iron.

4 Turn fabric right side out and stuff with fiberfill. Sew pillow closed with hand-sewing needle and matching thread.

5 *Optional:* Make throw pillows with leftover floral-print fabric following steps 3 and 4 and using smaller pieces of fabric.

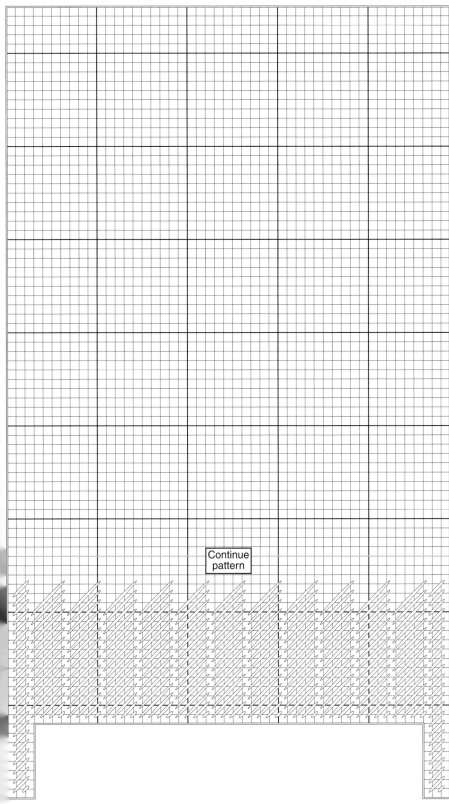

Continue pattern

Armoire Back
49 holes x 85 holes
Cut 1 from 7-count
Stitch with yarn

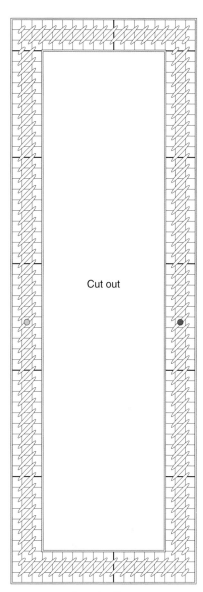

Cut out

Armoire Door
18 holes x 53 holes
Cut 2 from 7-count
Stitch with yarn

COLOR KEY	
Yards	**Medium Weight Yarn**
350 (320m)	☐ White #311
90 (82.3m)	▦ Lavender #358
50 (45.7m)	☐ Frosty green #661
	Uncoded areas on 7-count are white Continental Stitches
	✎ Lavender #358 Backstitch
	6-Strand Embroidery Floss
20 (18.3m)	☐ White (12 plies)
12 (11m)	▦ Dark blue violet #3746 (12 plies)
3 (2.8m)	✎ Very light pistachio green #369 Backstitch (12 plies)
	◯ Attach bead to right door
	● Attach bead to left door

Color numbers given are for Red Heart Super Saver Art. E300 medium weight yarn and DMC 6-strand embroidery floss.

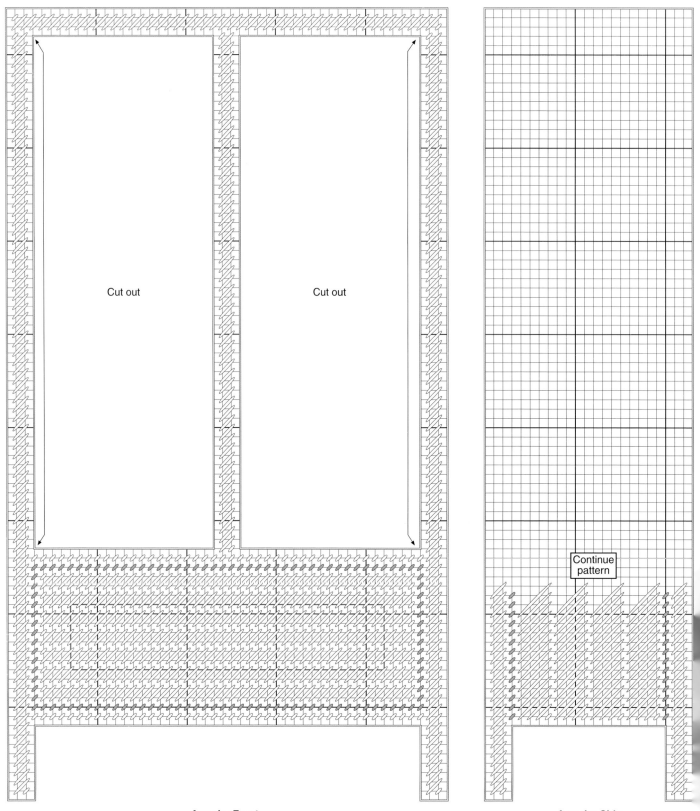

Armoire Front
49 holes x 85 holes
Cut 1 from 7-count
Stitch with yarn

Armoire Side
23 holes x 85 holes
Cut 2 from 7-count
Stitch with yarn

Cut out

Cut out

Continue
pattern

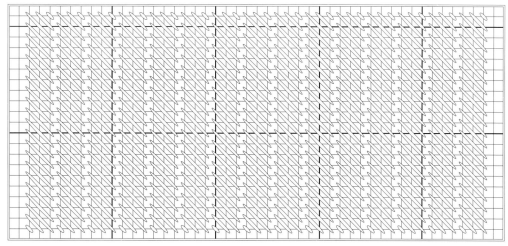

Armoire Inside Shelf
48 holes x 22 holes
Cut 1 from 7-count
Stitch with yarn

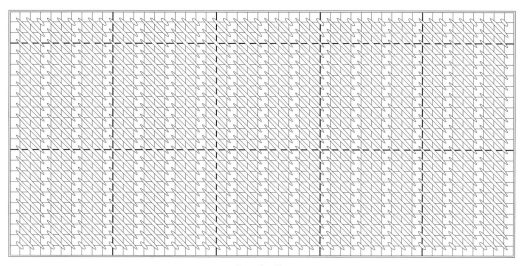

Armoire Top
49 holes x 23 holes
Cut 1 from 7-count
Stitch with yarn

Armoire Pole Bracket
7 holes x 5 holes
Cut 8 from 7-count
For each of the 2 brackets, place
4 pieces together and stitch as 1
Stitch with yarn

COLOR KEY

Yards	Medium Weight Yarn
350 (320m)	☐ White #311
90 (82.3m)	▨ Lavender #358
50 (45.7m)	☐ Frosty green #661
	Uncoded areas on 7-count
	are white Continental Stitches
	╱ Lavender #358 Backstitch
	6-Strand Embroidery Floss
20 (18.3m)	☐ White (12 plies)
12 (11m)	▨ Dark blue violet #3746 (12 plies)
3 (2.8m)	╱ Very light pistachio green
	#369 Backstitch (12 plies)
	◦ Attach bead to right door
	● Attach bead to left door

Color numbers given are for Red Heart Super Saver
Art. E300 medium weight yarn and DMC 6-strand
embroidery floss.

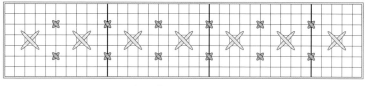

Armoire False Drawer
35 holes x 7 holes
Cut 1 from 7-count
Stitch with yarn

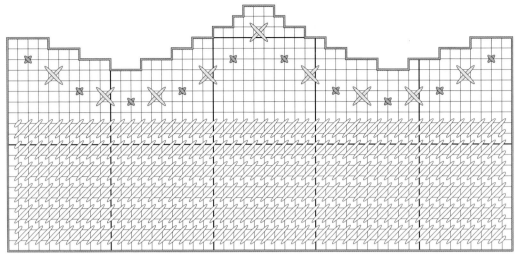

Footboard
49 holes x 23 holes
Cut 2 from 7-count
Stitch with yarn

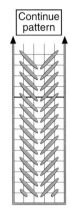

Canopy Top Side
5 holes x 85 holes
Cut 2 from 7-count
Stitch with yarn

Canopy Top End
5 holes x 49 holes
Cut 2 from 7-count
Stitch with yarn

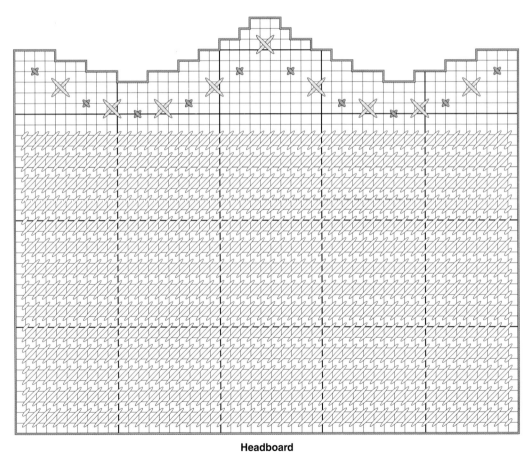

Headboard
49 holes x 39 holes
Cut 2 from 7-count
Stitch with yarn

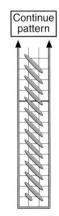

Canopy Inner Side
3 holes x 85 holes
Cut 2 from 7-count
Stitch with yarn

Canopy Inner End
3 holes x 49 holes
Cut 2 from 7-count
Stitch with yarn

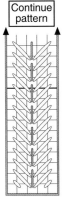

Continue pattern

Bedpost
5 holes x 89 holes
Cut 16 from 7-count
Stitch with yarn

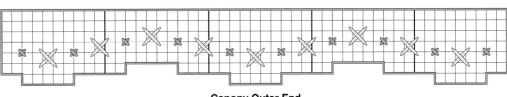

Canopy Outer End
49 holes x 7 holes
Cut 2 from 7-count
Stitch with yarn

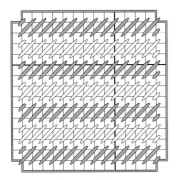

Square Pillow
15 holes x 15 holes
Cut 4 from 7-count
Stitch 2 with yarn as graphed
Stitch 2 replacing
white with lavender

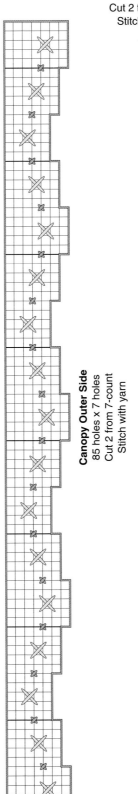

Canopy Outer Side
85 holes x 7 holes
Cut 2 from 7-count
Stitch with yarn

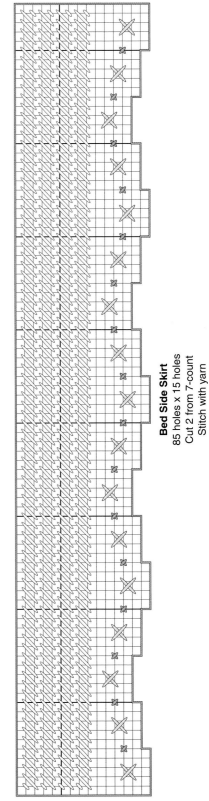

Bed Side Skirt
85 holes x 15 holes
Cut 2 from 7-count
Stitch with yarn

COLOR KEY

Yards	Medium Weight Yarn
350 (320m)	☐ White #311
90 (82.3m)	▨ Lavender #358
50 (45.7m)	☐ Frosty green #661
	Uncoded areas on 7-count are white Continental Stitches
	⟋ Lavender #358 Backstitch

6-Strand Embroidery Floss

20 (18.3m)	☐ White (12 plies)
12 (11m)	▨ Dark blue violet #3746 (12 plies)
3 (2.8m)	⟋ Very light pistachio green #369 Backstitch (12 plies)
	◯ Attach bead to right door
	● Attach bead to left door

Color numbers given are for Red Heart Super Saver Art. E300 medium weight yarn and DMC 6-strand embroidery floss.

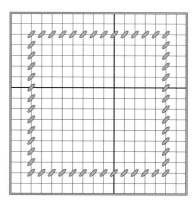

Nightstand Top
17 holes x 17 holes
Cut 1 from 7-count
Stitch with yarn

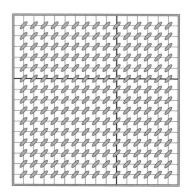

Nightstand Shelf
16 holes x 16 holes
Cut 1 from 7-count
Stitch with yarn

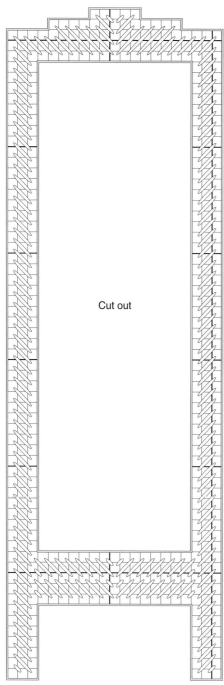

Cut out

Dressing Screen Panel
21 holes x 63 holes
Cut 6 from 7-count
Stitch with yarn

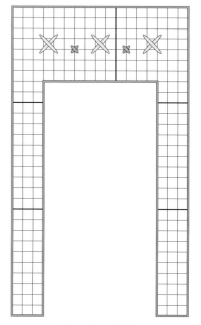

Nightstand Side
17 holes x 29 holes
Cut 4 from 7-count
Stitch with yarn

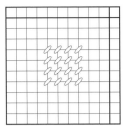

Lampshade Support
11 holes x 11 holes
Cut 1 from 10-count
Stitch with embroidery floss

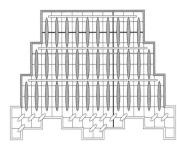

Lampshade
16 holes x 12 holes
Cut 4 from 10-count
Stitch with embroidery floss

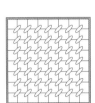

Lamp Base
8 holes x 8 holes
Cut 2 from 10-count
Stitch as 1
with embroidery floss

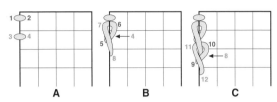

Braided Overcast Stitch
Work first two Overcast stitches
as shown in graph A
Following graph B, begin working braid by
wrapping yarn around back of canvas from 4 to 5,
then bring needle up to 6, around
back of canvas to 7 and down at 8
Following graph C, continue
working braid, covering entire edge

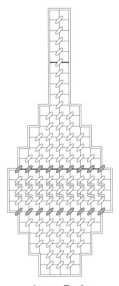

Lamp Body
10 holes x 25 holes
Cut 4 from 10-count
Stitch with embroidery floss

COLOR KEY	
Yards	**Medium Weight Yarn**
350 (320m)	☐ White #311
90 (82.3m)	▨ Lavender #358
50 (45.7m)	☐ Frosty green #661
	Uncoded areas on 7-count are white Continental Stitches
	⁄ Lavender #358 Backstitch
	6-Strand Embroidery Floss
20 (18.3m)	☐ White (12 plies)
12 (11m)	▨ Dark blue violet #3746 (12 plies)
3 (2.8m)	⁄ Very light pistachio green #369 Backstitch (12 plies)
	○ Attach bead to right door
	● Attach bead to left door

Color numbers given are for Red Heart Super Saver Art. E300 medium weight yarn and DMC 6-strand embroidery floss.

The full line of The Needlecraft Shop
products is carried by Annie's Attic catalog.
TOLL-FREE ORDER LINE
or to request a free catalog
(800) 582-6643
Customer Service
(800) 449-0440
Visit AnniesAttic.com

We have made every effort to ensure the accuracy
and completeness of these instructions. We cannot,
however, be responsible for human error, typographical
mistakes or variations in individual work.

ISBN: 978-1-57367-335-8

Printed in USA

1 2 3 4 5 6 7 8 9

Getting Started

Before You Cut

Buy one brand of canvas for each entire project as brands can di[f]fer slightly in the distance between bars. Count holes carefully from t[he] graph before you cut, using the bolder lines that show each 10 hole[s] These 10-count lines begin in the lower left corner of each graph [to] make counting easier. Mark canvas before cutting; then remove all mar[ks] completely before stitching. If the piece is cut in a rectangular or squa[re] shape and is either not worked, or worked with only one color a[nd] one type of stitch, the graph is not included in the pattern. Instead, t[he] cutting and stitching instructions are given in the general instructions with the individual project instructions.

Covering the Canvas

Bring needle up from back of work, leaving a short length of yarn [on] back of canvas; work over short length to secure. To end a thread, wea[ve] needle and thread through the wrong side of your last few stitches; cl[ip.] Follow the numbers on the small graphs beside each stitch illustration; bri[ng] your needle up from the back of the work on odd numbers and down throu[gh] the front of the work on even numbers. Work embroidery stitches last, af[ter] the canvas has been completely covered by the needlepoint stitches.

Shopping for Supplies

For supplies, first shop your local craft
and needlework stores. Some supplies
may be found in fabric, hardware and
discount stores. If you are unable to find
the supplies you need, please call Annie's
Attic at (800) 582-6643 to request a free
catalog that sells plastic canvas supplies.

Basic Stitches

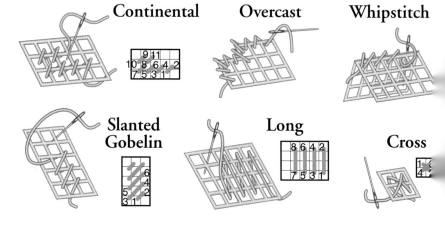

Continental • Overcast • Whipstitch • Slanted Gobelin • Long • Cross

Embroidery Stitches

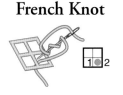

French Knot

Lazy Daisy

Backstitch

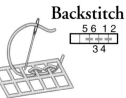

Straight

METRIC KEY:
millimeters = (mm)
centimeters = (cm)
meters = (m)
grams = (g)